There is a Love

For God *so* loved. . .   JOHN 3:16

"Beside pure love all other uncountable variations of what is called love and to be loved fade."

God is love, and love lives where God is let in.

And now I will show you the best way of all.
I may speak in tongues of men or of angels, but if I
am without love, I am a sounding gong or a clanging
cymbal. I may have the gift of prophecy, and know
every hidden truth; I may have faith strong enough
to move mountains; but if I have no love, I am
nothing. I may dole out all I possess, or even give my
body to be burnt, but if I have no love, I am none
the better.
Love is patient; love is kind and envies no one. Love
is never boastful, nor conceited, nor rude; never
selfish, not quick to take offence. Love keeps no score
of wrongs; does not gloat over other men's sins, but
delights in the truth. There is nothing love cannot
face; there is no limit to its faith, its hope, and its
endurance.
Love will never come to an end.

                                                    PAUL

Wear me as a seal upon your heart,
as a seal upon your arm;
for love is strong as death,
passion cruel as the grave;
it blazes up like blazing fire,
fiercer than any flame.
Many waters cannot quench love,
no flood can sweep it away;
if a man were to offer for love
the whole wealth of his house,
it would be utterly scorned.

                    SONG OF SOLOMON

Love worketh no ill to his neighbour; therefore love *is* the
fulfilling of the law.

                                                    PAUL

"YEA, I HAVE LOVED THEE WITH AN EVERLASTING LOVE: THEREFORE WITH LOVING-KINDNESS HAVE I DRAWN THEE." JER 31:3

O Jesus Christ's crown of thorns.
That has more wisdom than this world can give.
O great blessedness, O mysteriousness
and every sin You can forgive.

I swear you faithfulness, humility
and obedience to the end.
From this day to eternity
My destiny is in your hand.

Now all my sin you reconciled
my heart can cry of happiness.
You are my Lord — I am your bride.
Great mystery of blessedness!

Sven Lidman

There is a Love

Birgitta Yavari

Photo: Fred Denouden

To Fatima and to you
who hunger spiritually,
with the hope this
book will bring about
some of the love this
world cannot give.
Joh. 3:16   Zep. 3:17

LOGOS INTERNATIONAL

PLAINFIELD, NEW JERSEY, 1972

© 1972 by Interbook Publishing AB
All rights reserved
First published in Sweden by Bonniers under the title of
"Det finns en kärlek"
English translation by Lars Dunberg and Birgitta Yavari
Produced by Interbook Publishing AB, Box 3159, 103 63 Stockholm 3
Printed in Sweden by Esselte AB, Stockholm
ISBN 0-88270-005 hardcover; ISBN 0-88270-006 paperback

A wind now over the earth is blowing to all who hear and obey His word
He fills until overflowing God's Spirit, the Comforter

    Spirit sweet, come to me, so I'll be one with you
    Spirit sweet, I want to live with you, come and mould me
    Yes mould me, so I can give my life to you.

He doesn't follow our patterns. He doesn't take our advice.
He looks to a mind that's honest and gives out just by grace.

Ingamay

Whosoever therefore shall be ashamed of
me and of my words in this adulterous
and sinful generation: of him also shall
the Son of man be ashamed when he
cometh in the glory of his Father with
the holy angels.   Mark. 8:38

The Scriptures tell us
that bread won't feed
men's souls; obedience
to every word of God
is what we need.

MATT. 4:4

The truth shall make you free. JESUS

All power is given unto me in heaven and in earth.

Go ye therefore, and teach all nations, baptizing them in the name of the Father, and of the Son, and of the Holy Ghost.

Teaching them to observe all things whatsoever I have commanded you:

And, lo, I am with you always, **even** unto the end of the world.

Jesus

. . . As many as received him, to them gave he power to become the sons of God, **even** to them that believe on his name.

John. 1:12

He was the Love

Sometimes I'm walking around only thinking,
I'm often thinking of a lonesome man.
He walked around this world, a total stranger
He was true love, this extraordinary man.

A small crowd ever faithful went with Him.
And listened to His challenging mild voice.
He gave them rest and comfort in their turmoil,
and they followed Him by their own choice.

He was so humble and calm when it happened
He said only: Father, forgive them, what they've done
Then it was quiet, His agony was over.
It was all accomplished by our friend sublime.

Where'er He came, He spoke of God's love for us
He was so noble, so pure and true and fine.
But loud the people shouted: Crucify Him!
By great love He died the death that was mine.

Sometimes I'm walking around only thinking,
Often thinking of a lonesome man.
He walked around this world, a total stranger
He was true love, this extraordinary man.

Ingamay

WORDS AND MUSIC: INGAMAY HÖRNBERG

It's not a question of what we intend with God — but what God intends with us.
George Scott

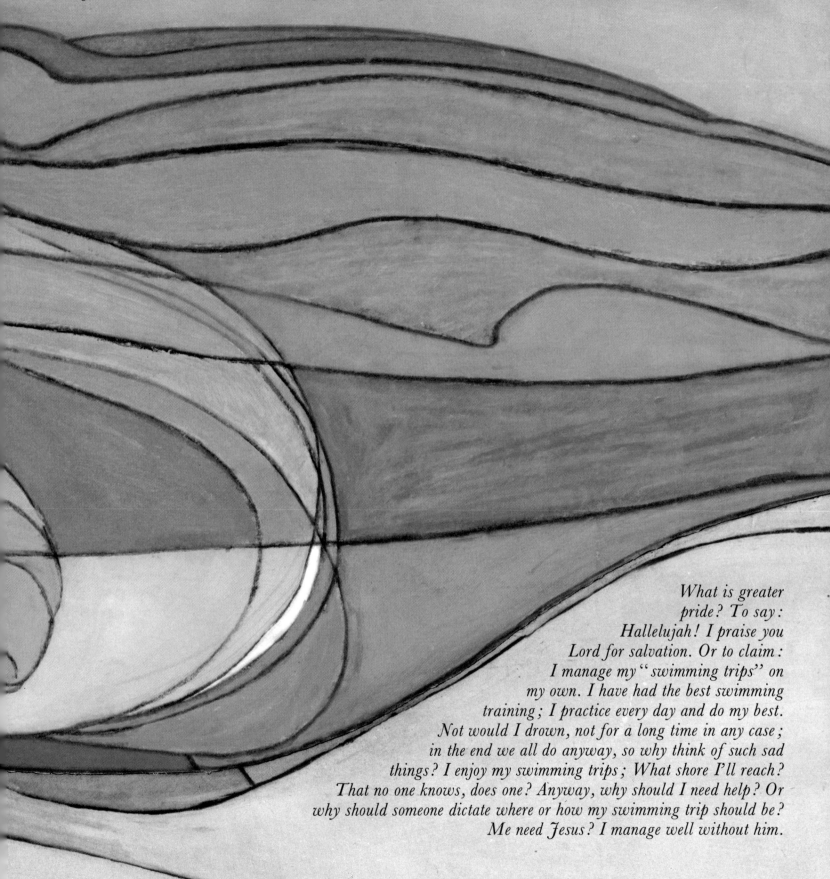

I was swimming at sea and realized that I wouldn't manage much longer. I cried for help. Someone heard me and took me up into his boat. If I then in my overwhelming joy and gratefulness would talk about what a fantastic salvation I received through my Helper, you then call me conceited and arrogant?

What is greater pride? To say: Hallelujah! I praise you Lord for salvation. Or to claim: I manage my " swimming trips " on my own. I have had the best swimming training; I practice every day and do my best. Not would I drown, not for a long time in any case; in the end we all do anyway, so why think of such sad things? I enjoy my swimming trips; What shore I'll reach? That no one knows, does one? Anyway, why should I need help? Or why should someone dictate where or how my swimming trip should be? Me need Jesus? I manage well without him.

Yours Eternally

Jesus, You most beautiful,
You the very purest one,
Who ever lived here on earth.
How great You are!
Thank You for Your love so full,
Thank You for Your sacrifice.
You for me was crucified,
To save my soul.
Jesus right now You see me.
You know I do need You.
Jesus, I want to be Yours forever!

When my strength is gone from me
I know that You see my needs,
And with peace and happiness
I leave it all to You.
You have promised that one day
I can come to You and stay.
Until then You are my guide
Lead me on Your way.
Thank You for Your love to me
You are all I ever need
Jesus, I want to be Yours eternally.

Ingamay

WORDS AND MUSIC: INGAMAY HÖRNBERG

Je-sus, you most beautiful, you the ve-ry pu-rest one
that ev-er lived here on earth. How great you are!
Thank you for your love so full. Thank you for your sa-cri-fice.
You for me were cru-ci-fied to save— my soul.
Jesus right now you see me. You know I do need you.
Jesus, I want to be yours for e————ver.

*...No, to Him I want to belong forever and say: Yours!
For Your will is my destiny! Dedicated! For my destiny
is to be united with You and used according to Your will.*

HE SENT FROM ABOVE,
HE TOOK ME:
HE DREW ME OUT
OF MANY WATERS:
HE DELIVERED ME . . .
2. Sam. 22:17

Show Me, Oh Lord, Your Way!

Lord help me to walk the way
That you've prepared just for me
I am so powerless and weak in myself
Show me, oh Lord, your way.

When all seems hard, the road is so long
You give me power, turn my woe into song
For burning wounds you give healing and care
When I reach you in prayer.

You have saved me, you have freed me
And in the midst of me I hear your voice
Take now my life and form it so
That I may go to heaven.

WORDS AND MUSIC: INGAMAY HÖRNBERG

*I hope that you can use this song, and that it will be a
blessing both for you, dear Birgitta, and for those who listen.*

*With love,
Ingamay*

I will instruct thee
and teach thee
in the way
which thou shalt go:
I will guide thee
with mine eye.

PSALM 32:8

Lord, don't let anything bind those dear wings
That once by mercy You gave unto me
Make me detached from all earthly things
That I may sing and live happy for Thee.

Evil snares lay down here on the ground,
Over them I hurriedly roam,
Grant that I never in them may be found
When on the way to my heavenly home.
Lina Sandell

"My boat is a small one,
The sea so big,
But Jesus takes hold of my hand.
He's steering the boat,
And I fear no more,
When we travel home to his land."

"What does it profit a man if he,
With full sails
And with the wind of admiration
And cheering, travels through the world
But becomes a wreck on the coast of eternity?"

*

For what is a man profited, if he
shall gain the whole world, and lose
his own soul? or what shall a man
give in exchange for his soul?

JESUS

I will follow you, my Jesus,
Follow you, where'er You go,
Follow on the sunlit mountain,
Or through the dark below.
I will follow on the right road
Where your feet have trod before;
Every step will bring me closer
To your home for evermore.

May I never ask the question,
Lord, where are you leading me.
Never filled with fear and doubting,
For you know my destiny.
No, I only have to follow,
Never choose the path or road
But in a childlike way obey you
travelling to your abode.

But if something is binding me
With just a slender band,
And to me will be a hindrance.
For my journey to your land,
Make me free, yea, free in my spirit,
Free to follow happily,
Free to love you, free to serve you,
Know your sweet will is for me.

Take my will and all my passions,
Take me in your will divine.
When I'm tired of the journey
Whisper to me: You are mine.
If you followed me in this world,
During years so filled with woe,
You will follow me forever
Follow me where'er I go.

Lina Sandell

When someone becomes a Christian he becomes
a brand new person inside.

2 Cor. 5:17

Where are you going . . .

That if thou shalt confess
with thy mouth the Lord Jesus,
and shalt believe in thine heart
that God hath raised him
from the dead,
thou shalt be saved.

For with the heart
man believeth unto
righteousness:
and with the mouth
confession is made
unto salvation.

Paul to the Romans

. . **Where are you going,** yes I'm wond'ring to where your way leads?
You've been searching all the world around, maybe you are searching even now.
You're searching for happiness, but you still haven't found it,
and sometimes you say: To where leads my way?
Now I'm also wondering: To where leads your way? Where are you going . . .

Does my question to you seem too repetious? I only want to make you understand
how important it is, that you think of to where you are going.
For just think: One day you can not choose again. Where are you going . . .

Ingamay

I want to tell you of a friend I have, a friend who's more dear to me than all on earth.
I love Him and He's loving me, that's what He said and I believe His word.

When I am lonely, and everyone has forgotten me, I have my friend who so faithfully stands by.
He is the only one who never condemned me. He gives me love and peace every day.

This friend is Jesus, God's own dear Son. The glory of heaven He left behind.
Because He so loved everyone on earth. He wanted to give eternal life.

In order to save us to eternal life He let Himself be nailed to a cross and die.
That was a hard step, but He took it for our sake. Because He so loved with love pure as snow!

How can then anyone deny this friend. He, only He, can give room in heaven.
No one understands like Him, no one like Him, no one is like my Jesus!

Ingamay

Dear friends,
let us practice loving each other
for love comes from God
and those who
are loving and kind
show that they are
the children of God
and that they are getting to
know Him better
(apostel John)

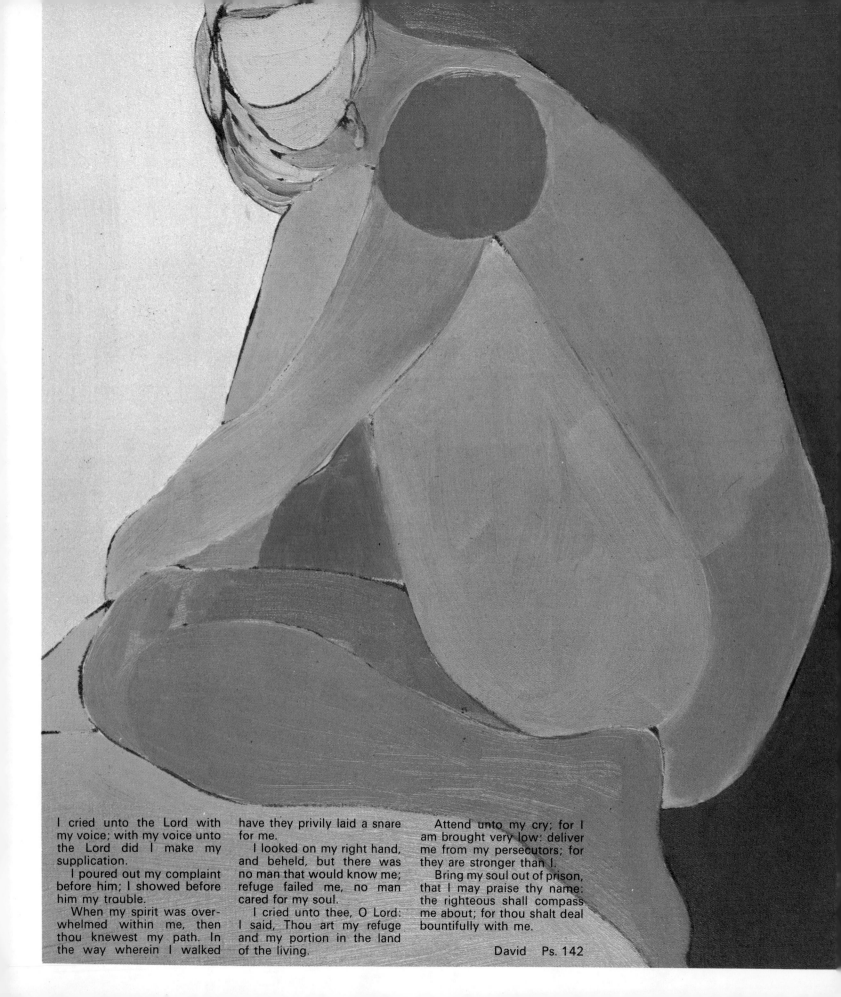

I cried unto the Lord with my voice; with my voice unto the Lord did I make my supplication.

I poured out my complaint before him; I showed before him my trouble.

When my spirit was overwhelmed within me, then thou knewest my path. In the way wherein I walked have they privily laid a snare for me.

I looked on my right hand, and beheld, but there was no man that would know me; refuge failed me, no man cared for my soul.

I cried unto thee, O Lord: I said, Thou art my refuge and my portion in the land of the living.

Attend unto my cry; for I am brought very low: deliver me from my persecutors; for they are stronger than I.

Bring my soul out of prison, that I may praise thy name: the righteous shall compass me about; for thou shalt deal bountifully with me.

David   Ps. 142

There's a land with always sunshine.
There's a land with eternal spring.
There's a land where no one's crying.

In that land there lives my Jesus.
He went there to stay.
Now He is before the Father,
for our sake to speak and pray.

In my Bible I can read that
There it's not at all like here.
No more weeping, no more worries.
No more suffering, no fear.

No, that place has not its likeness.
Will it be your destiny?
If you give your life to Jesus
You'll have a great eternity.

Ingamay

Jesus of Nazareth walks along here as he once did long ago,
Frees all those captured by sin and fear, he lets his peace and mercy flow:
God's own kingdom is near.

To the poor ones he gives his wealth, the fettered he will set free.
Those who were beaten are given health, and share in his liberty:
God's own kingdom is near.

Open your heart in repentance and prayer, open every secret door.
Jesus, God's Son, for you will care, just trust him for ever more:
God's own kingdom is near.

Anders Frostenson

Come to the Water (Jesuspeople)

Jesus I give you my heart and my soul.
I know that without God I'll never be whole.
Savior, I woke up, Father I adore
and I thank you and I praise you from earth's humble shores,
take me I'am yours!

And Jesus said: "Come to the water, stand by my side.
I know you are thirsty, you won't be denyed.
I felt every teardrop when in darkness you cried
and I strove to remind you that for those tears I died.

Jesuspeople

"*Just as ordinary free church people*"

efore it was LSD and heroin   Now they are called the JESUS people

And let him that is athirst
come. And whosoever will, let him
take the water of life freely.

JESUS

To Nietzsche:

"MY GOD
IS NOT DEAD.
SORRY ABOUT
YOURS"

"When we consider the universe as a whole, reason refuses to look upon it as a result of chance"   *Charles Darwin*

God does not die the day
when we cease to believe
in a personal deity,
but we die the day
when our lives cease to be
illuminated by the radiance,
renewed daily, of a miracle,
from sources beyond
all human reason.
Dag Hammarskjöld

TODAY IS THE FIRST DAY OF THE REST OF YOUR LIFE!

Jesus, reveal Yourself to those who are seeking but are hindered by the intellectual barriers of denial and doubting of our time. Touch someone who is not even aware of his or her spiritual hunger, to long for the heavenly nourishment and Your fellowship.

Jesus, give someone courage to ask for You and Your love, help someone to understand that without You the judgement remains: " You shall surely die". Help someone to humble himself, to break his pride and say " Jesus, You who have all power in heaven and on earth, forgive me all my sins and most of all for turning my back on You".

Cleanse me in Your blood, that flowed for me at Calvary and help my poor faith and to understand the fact that You were sacrificed as a lamb of atonement for the whole world on the cross and let me now experience the power thereof and help me to so walk that I as a gift may receive the Holy Spirit.

Thank You Jesus, for salvation, in Your name   Amen

Six thousand years of recorded history has to me proved that the greatest politicians and philosophers together in the world and history have not managed to re-establish any paradise.

The most important stand is neither political nor philosophical but for or against You, Jesus, the only one able to save and change our innermost being. For the problem is not the atom bomb but the human heart. And that's where the revolution ought to start. We need more bread and clothing for brothers in our world, but first of all more people born again by God's Spirit to change misery into paradise.

You think you can keep a few trivial things,
That God doesn't need to have all,
But don't forget that: Many who listen and see
they know when a Christian is cold.

You must be freed from it all,
Otherwise Jesus can't use you.
Your sins, your passions, yes, all
That stops you from walking his way.

My friend, when you stand before God's throne one day,
And life on this earth is done,
Consider if your life has hindered someone
To seek to come closer to God.

Well, come now, while God still is waiting for you,
He can start again in your life,
And through your new life He wants to show the world
That He, only He, can give peace.

Ingamay

He takes your sins, the worst you're possessing, and gives you his best now and forever. Sören Jansson

"Young or maybe old. It makes no difference.
Colored or just white. It makes no difference.
Poor or maybe rich. It makes no difference.
We all need each other now.

Give me your hand, we've the same road to walk.
Give me your hand, we've the same goal to reach.
Let's leave the difference, and let's think his way.
We all need each other now.

Our poor world is scattered now as never before.
We crawl into our shelters and close our door.
Over separating walls you hear once more.
We all need each other now."

For that which would unite us is so much greater than that which would separate us!

God Knows It All

My Lord is so good, He cares for my life.
When all gets me down, He helps in my strife.
He's faithful and trusting and loving to me.
What He's done for you He wants you to see.

God knows it all, the burdens you bear.
God knows it all, sorrow you can't share.
He knows the pain and grief that burn within your soul
He knows it all and He can make you whole.

My Lord is eternal, has almighty power
And life's many questions He will for you solve.
When you feel condemned and your life is to blame,
just know, up in heaven they know you by name.

My Lord He will help you and guide you along.
To walk in obedience, be steadfast and strong.
Dont fear, trust in God and in Jesus, His Son.
He will guide your steps till the battle is won.

Ingamay

WORDS AND MUSIC: INGAMAY HÖRNBERG

1. My Lord is so good, He — cares for my life. When
all gets me down, He — helps in my strife. He's
faithful and trusting and lov-ing to me. What
He's done for you He — wants you to see.

Chorus: God knows it all, the burdens that you bear.
God knows it all, the sorrow you can't share. He knows the
pain and grief that burn within your soul.
He knows it all and He can make you whole—.

Don't worry about anything; instead, pray about everything;
tell God your needs and don't forget to thank him for his answers.

If you do this you will experience God's peace, which is far more
wonderful than the human mind can understand. His peace will keep
your thoughts and your heart quiet and at rest as you trust
in Christ Jesus.

PAUL TO THE PHILIPPIANS

I Am Surely Not A Heathen

I am baptized and I am confirmed and I am surely not a heathen.
Sometimes I can go into a church when I want to find a little feelin.
But anyhow, the priests and pastors they do not live as they do teach,
They fight about doctrinal questions, 'bout sin and evil they do preach.

I do my best and mind my business and I give some money to the Red Cross.
I do not want to be a hypocrite who goes around condemning all the others.
The Christians think that they are saints and have such high morality.
But all the time they only argue: too many churches I can see.

I want to live my life just as I wish, I really have deserved that.
I am only a human so what more can then you from me demand?
When I get into my old age then I will think about my God.
I'll make it to his heaven easy, for isn't love Gods command?

When we're called into his kingdom we often want to escape him.
I was trying like that until I noticed: my old house was built on weak sand.
For other people's faults and shortcomings didn't give me my righteousness.
I stood there lonely for my Master, to pieces went my decentness.

The Lord said: You may come now for I see through all the fancy talking.
You can have eternal life and peace if you with me down here are walking.
And all the questions that seemed too big, decreased when he came in my heart.
Now he will never ever leave me, we'll never from each other part.

You who listen to my simple song, please consider your position.
Other people's customs, wrongs or your self-righteousness give no salvation.
Yea, here and now we choose our future, and what is called eternity.
To take the grace that Jesus gives us makes heaven a reality.

WORDS AND MUSIC: SVEN O. NILSSON

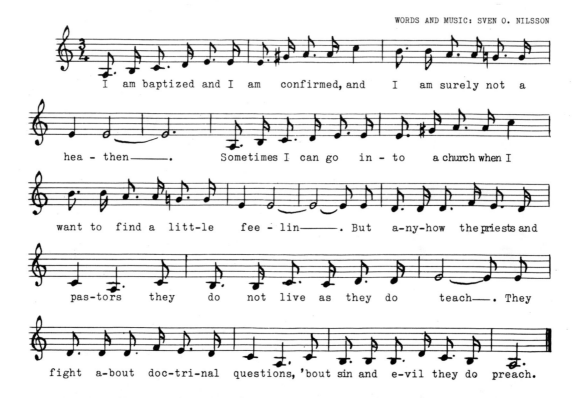

John 12:46—48

**You don't become wiser just because the years pass by.
But you've got the chance.**

Don't just fill your life with years
— fill the years with life!

I have come that you may have life and more than enough!

JESUS

We are not permitted to choose the frame for our destiny.
But what we put into it is ours.

Dag Hammarskjöld

THE GOSPEL ACCORDING TO

ST. JOHN

CHAPTER 1

IN the beginning was the Word, and the Word was with God, and the Word was God.

2 The same was in the beginning with God.

3 All things were made by him; and without him was not any thing made that was made.

4 In him was life; and the life was the light of men.

5 And the light shineth in darkness; and the darkness comprehended it not.

6 ¶ There was a man sent from God, whose name *was* John.

7 The same came for a witness, to bear witness of the Light, that all *men* through him might believe.

8 He was not that Light, but *was sent* to bear witness of that Light.

9 *That* was the true Light, which lighteth every man that cometh into the world.

10 He was in the world, and the world was made by him, and the world knew him not.

11 He came unto his own, and his own received him not.

12 But as many as received him, to them gave he power to become the sons of God, *even* to them that believe on his name:

13 Which were born, not of blood, nor of the will of the flesh, nor of the will of man, but of God.

14 And the Word was made flesh, and dwelt among us, (and we beheld his glory, the glory as of the only begotten of the Father,) full of grace and truth.

15 ¶ John bare witness of him, and cried, saying, This was he of whom I spake, He that cometh after me is preferred before me: for he was before me.

16 And of his fulness have all we received, and grace for grace.

17 For the law was given by Moses, *but* grace and truth came by Jesus Christ.

18 No man hath seen God at any time; the only begotten Son, which is in the bosom of the Father, he hath declared *him*.

en shall ye call
n me, and ye
l go and pray
o me, and I will
rken unto you.
d ye shall seek me,
l find *me*, when
hall search for me
h all your heart.
d I will be found
ou, saith the Lord.

JER. 29:12—14

Peace I leave with you, my peace I give unto you: not as the world giveth give I unto you.

Jesu

When He led my soul from darkness to light, I received peace—peace that this world cannot give.

From a world that none of us
sees God's Spirit comes to us and
a miracle happens. Frostenson

hope dwell in your breast.

JESUS KRISTUS
DITT ENDA HOPP

But seek ye first the
kingdom of God, and
his righteousness: and
all these things shall
be added unto you.
Matt. 6:33

FAITH
HOPE
LOVE
AND THE GREATEST OF THESE
IS LOVE

OUR REAL HOME IS LOVE

But as it is written, Eye hath not
seen, nor ear heard, neither have
entered into the heart of man,
the things which God hath prepared
for them that love him.

1 Cor. 2:9

Let Us All Once Reunite

Chorus:
Let us all once reunite
in our glorious home above

Have you thought of that our life
Here on earth will come to end?
Every one that's loving Jesus
Will move home with him, my friend.

I have had so many friends
Who too soon have passed away.
I felt grief but not for long
Because we'll meet again some day.

My dear friend, don't you want to meet
Your dear ones home above?
You will be close to Jesus
and never ever apart again.

Ingamay

WORDS: INGAMAY HÖRNBERG   MUSIC: AM. TRAD.

Chorus:
Let us   all once re - u - nite   in our

glorious home   a-bove. Let us   all once   re-u-

nite—   in our glorious home   a - bove.

1. Have you thought of   that our   life here   on—

earth will come   to end? Every   one that's loving

Je-sus will move home with him, my   friend.

Our lives either draw a line over or under our confession.   Fredrik Wislöff

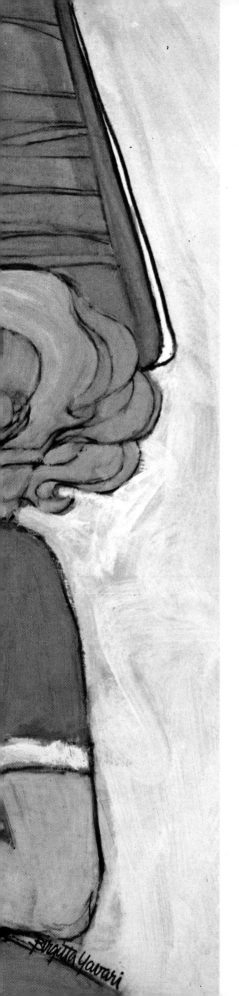

Love is such a misused and distorted word.
No one can force his love on someone — neither
does God force His love on us — but if
we let it in, it is so strong that it can change
our hearts and transform our lives.

Without holiness no man shall see the Lord.

HEB. 12:14

Solveig Andersson
pallas film

EVA
THE FIRST STONE

COLOR!

My beloved sister,

Wounds that burn purify — and you know, God doesn't want everything that happens to happen but He wants something with us in that which does happen. The finest fruit doesn't ripen only by sunshine, does it Solveig? No, the best apples, for example, should preferable' have a night of frost before harvest.

I do wish you would feel — in spite of what life recently has given you, and just in time for your birthday, of disappointment and loss — that you are loved. Not just by your close ones here, but most of all; that God loves you, that Jesus loves you — with a love so powerful that when we let it in, it changes hearts and transforms life! — that we are loved, not because we are worth it, but because it is in the nature of God. God has revealed Himself to us, sacrificed Himself, crucified our guilt and all our failures and reconciled Himself with us through Jesus.

And to emphasize, but with a slightly different content that you are not alone, I will quote some words of a thinker: "When you have locked your door and turned off the light in your room, don't say you are alone, for you are not." No, for me the unseen together with the seen and measurable form reality, and the former lies as foundation for the latter and is of eternal value and is worthy to be conscious of and live before. But also to be conscious of what part of the unseen you want to be acquainted with, influenced by and led by.

You know Solveig, through faith in God and the One He has sent (and not just faith in the sense that God exists, but to live in confidence of what God, who has not been silent nor passive in our history, has said, acted, given and fulfilled promises) we do gain restored personal relationship with our Creator and through Jesus we are washed clean and dressed in the garments of righteousness. We receive the peace that Jesus left behind, that passes all understanding, and participation in His Spirit!

Someone has said that life in this world often is a tragedy for those with feelings and a suffering for those who meet it with their hearts. But the great thing is, how naive it ever may seem, that Jesus wants to stay in our hearts, change and equip us and fill us with His presence. It is a temple of praise we were meant to own, instead of a receiver of suffering.

The love, joy and power I experience in Jesus I don't want to exchange for anything this world could ever offer.

No, I pray to be separated from all that separates me from the life with Jesus and I want to live so that I with Paul can say: "I myself no longer live, but Christ lives in me" and as John the Baptist: "He must increase and I must decrease," — that I more and more in the "workshop of God" am emptied of my own poor and dirty inside and with my senses turned and responsive to the pure love of Jesus. Because it is when my innermost being is enlightened and filled with the presence of Jesus that I taste a joy that gives me a foretaste of heaven, and I receive strength to be able to spread and share that which gives life meaning. Although life isn't always sunshine, and my faith isn't built upon my shifting emotional life, but foremost on the word of God and the promises of God, I have a sure foundation and can with trust see a meaning in and with all that happens. And I have, like Paul, received a great conviction that for those who love God everything will work for the best. At the same time, the discipleship has a price and it can cost something to own the miracle of salvation. Salvation is precious. We are eternal beings and our stand doesn't just hold consequences here and now but also where we are to spend eternity after our short life on earth.

Pascal writes: "Human things one must know in order to love. Divine things one must love in order to know." "God doesn't remain something abstract for those who really search Him. The Lord says through Jeremia that He wants to listen to us and He wants to let Himself be found, if we ask for Him with all our heart.

I finish with a strong wish that you, perhaps to your very birthday, through the power of faith, would experience the rebirth to a life for, with and by the Spirit of God.

with love in Jesus, Birgitta

There is
no great
art where
there is
no love

Isn't it as obvious that there is a creator to the creation, whereof we are a part, as there is an artist to every piece of art?

The piece of art is never superior to the artist.

God, give us humbleness before the fact that You have created us—and not we ourselves—and that You created man to Your image and not vice versa!

Although still I'm plauged by sorrow and by sin,
I am the bride of a mighty king.
Often may the want of faith the question bring:
Where is your garment and where is your ring?

Oh Jesus, open thou my eye
That I may see my riches here.
I have a Father up on high,
Who has for me a Father's care.

I have a brother who'll at my side abide,
And who for me is always praying.
An eternal grace as stretching wide,
As over me the sky I'm viewing.

Have you got courage to follow Jesus, will you to His followers belong?
Listen to another question asked here in a simple song:
Have you got courage not to be present when the King is drawing nigh?
Calling you to glorious blessing, calling you to His home on high.

Have you got courage to still go dreaming about fortune here on earth,
Though you often reaped its harvest, and you've seen how little it was worth?
All the riches soon get swift wings, flowers of pleasure fade away,
And you are tossed upon a wild sea, in this world you go astray.

Oh take heed, He still is calling: there is grace yet to be found.
Oh precious soul what's hindering you, in what snares have you been bound?
Listen to His Spirit calling, at the door of your heart He still is knocking.
Have you got courage to keep it closed till no more you hear Him calling?

Lina Sandell

Jesus said unto her,
Said I not unto thee,
that, if thou
wouldest believe,
thou shouldest see
the glory of God?
JOHN 11:40

Thy will be done
in earth as *it is* in heaven.

Lord, teach me to think before everything:
Thy will be done
make me so pure
that I may bring about
something of heaven here on earth.

IF YOU CAN
BELIEVE IN
JESUS YOU
ARE HIS
FRIEND

FATIMA

And Peter replied: "Each one of you must turn from sin, return to God and be baptized in the name of Jesus Christ for the forgiveness of your sins, then you also shall receive the gift of the Holy Spirit."

Acts 2:38

Hallelujah!

Hallelujah?
Yes.
Hallelujah. Now and forever.
But why such a language?
You must talk in such a way that men of our time understand what you mean.
Of course, that's why: Hallelujah.
Few are so incomprehensible as those who think they are experts in "talking to our time."
And few words are so comprehensible as hallelujah.
There are languages that are understood at all times. The language of love, of joy. One of the best words in that language is hallelujah.
In a real hallelujah there is both love and joy.
At the same time it is a provocation. That is why so many people are embarrassed by the word hallelujah. Or claim that it is ridiculous.
It irritates.
Indifferent and kind Christians can if necessary be accepted.
Manifestations of joy must be reserved for people watching hockey or football.
The name of the devil you can use often and loud.
Hallelujah irritates because it breaks the ordinary pattern. It makes people that prefer forms instead of naturalness frown.
Hallelujah—it is the divine crime of etiquette against the human squareness.
It is the challenge for those who worship a lifeless and dead God. Hallelujah.

Ivar Lundgren

Hallelujah is Hebrew and means: Praise the Lord.

The end of the road decides its character. There is a detailed map in the Bible of the road to salvation—of acts of faith and steps in obedience that lead to the full blessing, participation in the promises and restored personal relationship with our Creator.

With all the earnestness I possess I tell you this: Unless you are born again you can never get into the kingdom of God.

Unless one is born of water and the Spirit, he cannot enter the kingdom of God. Man can only reproduce human life, but the Holy Spirit gives new life from heaven, so don't be surprised at my statement that you must be born again!

Jesus

With water I baptize those who repent of their sins; but someone else is coming, far greater than I am, so great that I am not worthy to carry his shoes! He shall baptize you with the Holy Spirit and with fire.

John

Ask the flower in the valley
"Oh, where are you facing to?"
She will answer: "To the bright sun,
This is where I get my glow."

Our souls are just like flowers
that are turned toward the light
Oh, my Jesus, may our eyes be
turned to you, with all our might.
                    Lina Sandell

The Lord's prayer:
Our Father which art in heaven
Hallowed be thy name
Thy kingdom come
Thy will be done in earth,
as it is in heaven
Give us this day our daily bread
and forgive us our depts as we forgive our deptors
and lead us not into temptation
but deliver us from evil.
MATT. 6:9—13

Deliver us from evil:

The devil is not a little black figure with tail and horns but a hyper-intelligent power using all means to snare and to destroy. A Jack-of-all-trades, sometimes disguised as the angel of light, to serve the truth in imitation.

There's only one who is the way, the truth and the life — JESUS! For thine is the kingdom, and the power and the glory forever!

A-MEN

Love's open door

Chorus:
As wind and grass and sand upon the seashore
God's ' ve is like a home with an open door.

As wind and grass and sand upon the seashore
God's love is like a home with an open door.
We are free to live there freely to come and go
Free to tell God ''yes'' and free to tell him ''No''.

We look for freedom to be what we are
Freedom to be something nothing else can mar
Not an empty freedom, but a vision that is true—
Lands where trees and flowers bloom in every hue.

Yet we build so many kinds of walls
Each one, through the iron bars, to his neighbour calls.
Each joint built strongly, with many stones of fear
Each one's hard-clenched ego is his prison-gear.

Judge us, Oh Lord, Oh Saviour, set us free
Let your glad forgiveness heal our agony
For forgiveness reaches where'er your love is found
To all lands and nations in the world around.

This about spiritual families. . . I think we must
look upon each other in such a way that our
denominations become homes and not prison
camps. We are different families with different
temperaments and qualities, and one day we will
meet in the same city for we belong to the same
family. It is important that we do not limit God
and that we ask for grace to be led by the Spirit.
The congregation is not an exhibition with
finished art objects, but God's workshop, a studio
of the Lord. . . but what an exhibition God has
planned! Revelation 7:9—17. And everyone
wanting to be formed by a master — and doesn't
doubt his mastership — is welcome into the
fellowship.

THE MASTER IS COME,
AND CALLETH FOR THEE.
JOHN 11:28

Oh, that you would realize it!

Give me a good digestion, Lord,
and also something to digest.
Give me a healthy body, Lord,
and wisdom to make proper use of it.
Give me a mind which isn't heavy and grumbly,
Give me a bit of humor also, Oh, Lord
Give me the mercy to see some fun sometimes.
(Prayer in the Cathedral of
Chester, England)

A Letter From A Friend

I have not had many friends here
although many people know my name
but I know I always have a friend
who helps me through the struggle on the way.

In this world I cannot see his face
still I know he's more than human race
he's the fairest one ever lived on earth
just think, to have a friend who is like that.

Yes, I know he is the purest one
for I know he is the fairest one
He has never ever lived in sin
just think, to have a friend who is like that.

Are you lonely just as I have been
feeling helpless, weak and often mean?
Go to this friend Jesus, God's own son
he is enough and lasts for all of us.

WORDS AND MUSIC: INGAMAY HÖRNBERG

On The Road

Life SHALL have purpose!

Delight thyself also in the Lord: and he shall give thee the desires of thine heart.

Commit thy way unto the Lord: trust also in him: and he shall bring *it* to pass.

Psalm 37:4, 5

*God conceals himself from those who examine him
but reveals himself to those who search for him.*

PASCAL

JER. 29:12—14

And I say unto you: ask, and it
shall be given you: seak, and ye shall
find: knock, and it shall be opened
unto you.

JESUS

Prayer is not begging, nor is it communication with one's own self;
it is fellowship with God.
Only for those that pray, God can seem to be alive.

Harry Emerson Fosdick

Thou who art over us,
Thou who art one of us,
Thou who art —
also within us,
May I prepare the way for Thee,
May I thank Thee for all that shall fall to my lot,
May I also not forget the needs of others,
Keep me in Thy love,
As Thou wouldest that all should be kept in mine.
May everything in this my being be directed to Thy glory
and may I never despair.
For I am under Thy hand,
and in Thee is all power and goodness.

Give me a pure heart — that I may see Thee,
a humble heart — that I may hear Thee,
a heart of love — that I may serve Thee,
a heart of Faith — that I may abide in Thee

Dag Hammarskjöld

Create and keep within me, Lord, a dwelling for yourself — a pure heart.
Separate me from all that is separating me from You.
Empty me of all my unpurity and fill me with Your love,
and give me wisdom to use it wisely.
Keep me in humble boldness,
and with my first love to You, Jesus!

Jesus, be my Lord and leader,
thank You for giving me heavenly food when You use me,
I want to be Yours, dedicated.
Let every step, every action be with You, for You, of You,
for I have tasted the joy in You —
joy, peace, and love this world cannot give.

ARABIC WOMAN IN OLD JERUSALEM

THE EMPTY TOMB OF JESUS IN THE ROCK AT CALVARY.

Jesus said: "I am the good shepherd; the good shepherd giveth his life for the sheep." JOH. 10:11

SHALOM!

EP RIVER, MY HOME IS OVER JORDAN!"   ARABIC WOMAN AT A BAZAAR IN OLD TOWN.

USALEM GOD'S CITY OF GOLD, BRASS AND OF LIGHT. FOR YOUR GS I LIKE TO BE A HARP YOU."

WITH A VIEW OVER THE SEA OF TIBERIAS.

Shalom is the Israeli greeting of peace.

Israel! I am lying in my hotel room in Jerusalem trying to collect some of the overwhelming impressions that You, Lord, have let me receive today. Each day with You is filled with miracles — it is so great to live in fellowship with You, Jesus, and I thank You, my heavenly Father, for Your goodness toward me.

I cannot fully share how great it feels to tread on holy ground. To know that here You walked, just here; here You carried Your cross. Jesus, thank You for all You did for us. Thank You for letting me view something of what I walk in faith for. And thank You for the words in Genesis: "Stay as a stranger here in this land, I will be with You and bless You." My Lord, thank You for Your words: "Heaven and earth will disappear, but my words remain forever."

The time is ten to four, my first "night" in Jerusalem. I was awakened by a — well, what was it? My eyes started watering, my skin went goosey in a mixture of dread, fright, and an almost indescribable expectation to hear the voice of God echo over Jerusalem. A bang or an explosion made my whole body shake, my hands and fingertips vibrate. Thoughts rushed in terrific speed through my small human mind — why should people fight — "behold, I'm watching over my word — behold, then is Your redemption near." I remembered the day little Fatima was delivered to life on earth out of me; I thought how it must have been to be delivered myself to this life. What will not then the deliverance involve, the deliverance that is though our great hope in the midst of the assurance of God's day and the sorrow of wrath? "Who are the ones coming out of the great tribulation? — These are the ones that have washed themselves in the blood of the Lamb."

My Lord, give me a faith so powerful that no fear will ever get dominion over me. Oh Jesus, save the girl who is rooming with me. Help me to be a transparent instrument for You, my Jesus. You know everything inside me, thank You for being with me every day, every moment. Lord, I want to be Your belonging!

The Arabic night porter tried to calm us by explaining what it was all about, an explanation that we first found difficult to believe. We happened to be in the Ramadan, the holy month of fasting for the Moslems, when they are allowed to eat at night but have to fast during the day. The bangs that woke us up were fired every morning at sunrise during this month as a signal that the fast had begun. We had to try getting used to these bangs every night at three or four o'clock during our stay in Jerusalem.

A bit later, but far too early, I was awakened by uncounted car horns. But I rejoice in a divine singing concert from the birds outside my window. The sky is gray, but it is light outside and I think: Oh, glorious morning. We were told last night that our window is facing a cemetery, and I see beautiful green trees, a high wall, a hill, and the sky. There are two sparrows in a willow tree just above the window and after the excitement during last night I think of the words in Matthew: "Not one sparrow—what do they cost—two for a penny?— can fall to the ground without Your Father knowing it"

It didn't take long before the light gray sky turned completely summer blue. And now I am going to eat my first Israeli breakfast.

It's great to be here. Yesterday I wandered about in Old Town, bought myself a Star of David necklace. I feel so astonishingly nationalistic, I belong to Israel, God's people. I also went into a remarkable church. Yes, remarkable, I couldn't figure it out. There the tomb of Mary should have been, there was Calvary, there was the Cross thrown, there was the chapel of St. Helen, there was the orthodox part, there was the Roman Catholic part . . . Gaudiness in Masses, the smell of incense, and rattlings of all kinds, small glass cabinets with Saint this and Saint that, decorated with gifts of jewelry from "important" people in our world. I couldn't connect this with Jesus's own outward simplicity but spiritual greatness.

But a missionary couple took me to a place that I rather believe was Calvary and the tomb which is called the Garden Tomb. There was such a strong and fine spirit and simpleness. Just think, my hotel room window that faced a cemetery—that is Calvary which is now turned into a Moslem cemetery. The Garden of Gethsemane and the Church of All Nations, built on The Mount of Olives at the cave where Jesus taught his disciples, gave strong impressions too. But to sit inside the grave I believe Jesus was laid in, and to pray there, was an indescribable experience.

I have also been to the Dead Sea, to swim, a remarkable and marvelous experience indeed. I floated like a cork and had laughing fits—after my swim it felt as if I had taken a dose of strong tranquilizing or sleeping pills. It is said to be very healthy. Does it contain the chemicals that drowned Sodom and Gomorrah? It is remarkable salt in any case.

The Israelites sing the beautiful song "Jerusalem, God's city of gold" which came about during the Six-Day War.—God surely isn't passive in our history, "not does He who defends Israel sleep."

"We are back to your wells and to your marketplace
and we go down to the Dead Sea through Jericho.
Jerusalem, God's city of gold, of brass and of light
for your songs I would like to be a harp for you."

Yes beautiful city, incredibly rich in events! I have had an old wish fulfilled as well. I have been riding a camel on The Mount of Olives! And still another desired experience: to swim in the Jordan River where John baptized Jesus.

Hallelujah! My roommate experienced salvation the day before she was to go back to Sweden. It is so wonderful to see how God searches a person in spite of all her hindrances and "hide-outs" and in spite of the trials from the evil one to spoil the re-union. To experience how a soul is taken from darkness into light and into a peace which this world cannot give. Amen!

In the morning we went to the tomb of Jesus. It is looked after by a Dutch couple and is situated in a small garden, just as described in the Bible. We prayed inside the empty tomb, and Ann-Sofie received Jesus into her heart as her personal Savior and confessed Him. The greatest and most important decision we can take in life, to restore the intended personal fellowship with our Creator through our Savior.

Naturally I have not missed the Nativity Church in Bethlehem. One evening the missionary couple, myself, and two Norwegians studying theology and physics, travelled to visit a sister in the faith, Anette, at a kibbutz by the Dead Sea. As there was not room for us at the Sabbath evening meal in the huge dining hall, we set a table outside under the Israeli starry sky and celebrated a real love feast to the remembrance of Jesus, with wine and with hymns of praise.

BEAR YE ONE ANOTHER'S BURDENS AND SO FULFIL THE LAW OF CHRIST   PAUL

You carried Your cross, oh Jesus! for my sake You paid my price. Oh, that we all would understand what depth and what price You paid.

The most intellectual and intelligent cannot perhaps grasp the mystery of the cross, but the most simple and poor sinner can experience its power.

For the preaching of the cross is to them that perish foolishness: but unto us which are saved it is the power of God.
1 Cor. 1:18

And Jerusalem shall be trodden down of the Gentiles, until the times of the Gentiles be fulfilled.

And there shall be signs in the sun, and in the moon, and in the stars; and upon the earth distress of nations, with perplexity; the sea and the waves roaring;
Men's hearts failing them for fear, and for looking after those things which are coming on the earth: for the powers of heaven shall be shaken.

And then shall they see the Son of man coming in a cloud with power and great glory.

And when these things begin to come to pass, then look up, and lift up your heads; for your redemption draweth nigh.

. . . Heaven and earth shall pass away: but my words shall not pass away.   LUKE. 21:24—33

The prophet Isaiah writes in the Old testament about Jesus: The people that walked in darkness have seen a great light: they that dwell in the land of the shadow of death, upon them hath the light shined.   *Isaiah 9:2*

John writes in the New Testament: That was the true Light, which lighteth every man that cometh into the world. He was in the world, and the world was made by him, and the world knew him not. He came unto his own, and his own received him not. But as many as received him, to them gave he power to become the sons of God.

Isaiah prophesies further: For unto us a child is born, unto us a son is given; and the government shall be upon his shoulder: and his name shall be called Wonderful, Counseller, The mighty God, The everlasting Father, The Prince of Peace.

. . . For that which had not been told them shall they see: and that which they had not heard shall they consider. Who hath believed our report? And to whom is the arm of the Lord revealed? For he shall grow up before him as a tender plant, and as a root out of a dry ground. Surely he hath borne our griefs, and carried our sorrows: yet we did esteem him stricken, smitten of God, and afflicted. But he was wounded for our transgressions, he was bruised for our iniquities: the chastisement of our peace was upon him: and with his stripes we are healed. All we like sheep have gone astray: we have turned every one to his own way: and the Lord hath laid on him the iniquity of us all. He is brought as a lamb to the slaughter . . .   *Isaiah 53*

. . . But who among the people of today realize it was their sins he was dying for?

JESUS SAID UNTO HIM: I AM THE WAY, THE TRUTH, AND THE LIFE.

Herein is love, not that we loved God, but that he loved us, and sent his Son to be the propitiation for our sins.   *1 John 4:10*

To him give all the prophets witness, that through his name whosoever believeth in him shall receive remission of sins.   *Acts 10:43*

Jesus answered and said unto them, This is the work of God, that ye believe on him whom he hath sent.   *John 6:29*

He that believeth on the Son hath everlasting life: and he that believeth not the Son shall not see life; but the wrath of God abideth on him.   *John 3:36*

For other foundation can no man lay than that is laid, which is Jesus Christ.   *1 Cor. 3:11*

God watches over his own word, Jeremiah writes. The promises of the Old Covenant were fulfilled in the life, death and *resurrection* of Jesus! The promises of the New Covenant are valid for those who have circumsized their hearts in faith to Jesus. In over three hundred bible passages (our history written beforehand) there are promises concerning the second coming of Jesus, when He will come in royal power and glory as the Jews waited upon Him the first time.

When everything is ready, then I will come and get you, so that you always can be with me where I am. If this weren't so, I would tell you plainly.   *Jesus*

So stay awake and be prepared, for you do not know the date or moment of my return.   *Jesus*

Once like a hunted dove, as a wounded fawn I was,
but a deeply broken heart Jesus never has forsaken.

Fredrik Bloom

EVEN YOU BEING WELL OFF NEED JESUS

As no one is so unimportant that God doesn't have a plan for his life,
is neither anyone so gifted that his life wouldn't be a failure
if the plan of God isn't realized.

The closer we are to Jesus, the closer we are to each other.   *Mother Basilea*

We are one in the spirit
We are one in the Lord
And we pray that our unity
One day may be restored

And they'll know we are Christians by our love
Yes they'll know we are Christians by our love

All praise to the Father
From whom all things come
And all praise to Christ Jesus
His only Son
And all praise to the Spirit
Who makes us all one

I don't understand the power in the simple light bulb but I see the light. Lord, I don't see You with my eyes but You do reveal Yourself to my heart. And You let me experience the light, the power and the warmth of Your presence within me. Jesus, I want to be like the light bulb — pure, transparent and receptive.

"EXCEPT YE BE CONVERTED
AND BECOME AS LITTLE CHILDREN,
YE SHALL NOT ENTER INTO THE
KINGDOM OF HEAVEN." JESUS

The Lord is my shepherd; I shall not want.

. . . He maketh me to lie down in green pastures:
he leadeth me beside the still waters.
He restoreth my soul :
he leadeth me in the paths of righteousness
for his name's sake.

PSALM 23

Then shall the King say unto them on his right hand, Come, ye blessed of my Father, inherit the kingdom prepared for you from the foundation of the world: For I was an hungred, and ye gave me meat: I was thirsty, and ye gave me drink: I was a stranger and ye took me in: Naked, and ye clothed me: I was sick, and ye visited me: I was in prison, and ye came unto me.

Then shall the righteous answer him, saying, Lord, when saw thee an hungred, and fed thee? or thirsty and gave thee drink? When saw we thee a stranger, and took thee in? or naked, or clothed thee? Or when saw we thee sick, or in prison, and came unto thee?

And the King shall answer and say unto them, Verily I say unto you, Inasmuch as ye have done it unto one of the least of these my brethren, ye have done it unto me.

Then shall he say also unto them on the left hand, Depart from me, ye cursed, into everlasting fire, prepared for the devil and his angels: For I was an hungred, and ye gave me no meat: I was thirsty, and ye gave me no drink: I was a stranger, and ye took me not in: naked, and ye clothed me not: sick, and in prison, and ye visited me not.

Then shall they also answer him, saying, Lord, when saw we thee an hungred, or athirst, or a stranger, or naked, or sick, or in prison, and did not minister unto thee?

Then shall he answer them, saying, Verily I say unto you, Inasmuch as ye did it not to one of the least of these, ye did it not to me.

And these shall go away into everlasting punishment: but the righteous into life eternal.

I WAS HUNGRY,
and you set going a humanistic association,
and you discussed my hunger.
Thank you.

I WAS IN PRISON,
you sneaked quietly to your chapel
in the quiet neighbourhood,
and prayed for my liberation.

I WAS NAKED,
you wondered wasn't that perhaps unmoral?

I WAS ILL,
and you went on your knees
and praised God for your health.

I WAS HOMELESS,
you preached for me. About God's loving care.

I WAS LONESOME,
and you left me alone
to pray for me.
You seem so holy.
You seem so close to God.
But I am still hungry and lonesome
I'm freezing.
　　　　　　　　"Unknown"

Are we willing to pay the price of the discipleship?
Jesus, help understand that You call us to follow You and to serve You!

Lord, make me a tool for your peace,
Let me bring love, where hate reigns.
Let me bring forgiveness, where wrongs
have been committed.
Let me create harmony, where discord reigns,
Let me bring truth, where heresy reigns,
Let me bring hope where despair reigns,
Let me bring light, where darkness reigns,
Let me bring joy, where there is sorrow and distress.

Oh Master, do not let me so much seek
To be comforted as to comfort,
To be understood as to understand,
To be loved as to love,
It is through giving we get,
It is through forgetting ourselves
That we find ourselves.
It is when we forgive that we get forgiveness
And it is through dying that we are born to eternal life.
St. Francis

Come unto me, all ye that labour
and are heavy laden,
and I will give you rest.
Jesus

But whosoever drinketh of
the water that I shall give him
shall never thirst:
but the water that I shall
give him shall be in him
a well of water springing up
into everlasting life.
Jesus

Look! I have been standing
at the door and I am
constantly knocking.
If anyone hears me
calling him and opens
the door, I will come in
and fellowship with him
and he with me.

Jesus

People are like pianos
— they produce the
same tone you hit.

Therefore all things whatsoever
ye would that men should do to you,
do ye even so to them.

Jesus

Be thou faithful unto death,
and I will give thee a crown
of life.

Jesus

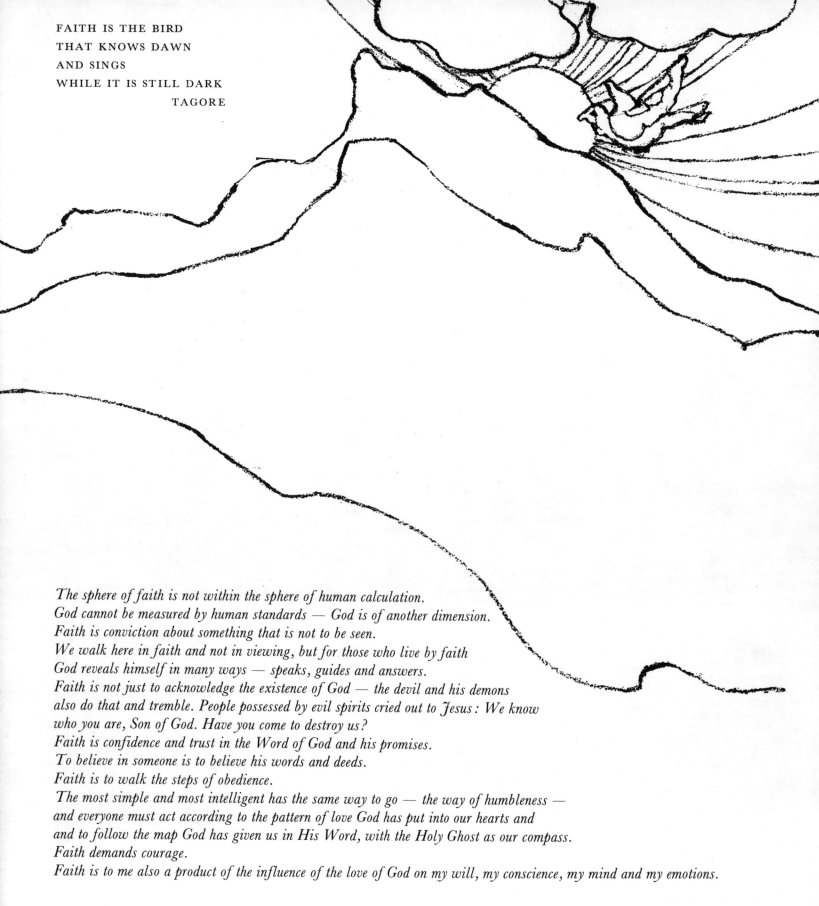

FAITH IS THE BIRD
THAT KNOWS DAWN
AND SINGS
WHILE IT IS STILL DARK
          TAGORE

The sphere of faith is not within the sphere of human calculation.
God cannot be measured by human standards — God is of another dimension.
Faith is conviction about something that is not to be seen.
We walk here in faith and not in viewing, but for those who live by faith
God reveals himself in many ways — speaks, guides and answers.
Faith is not just to acknowledge the existence of God — the devil and his demons
also do that and tremble. People possessed by evil spirits cried out to Jesus: We know
who you are, Son of God. Have you come to destroy us?
Faith is confidence and trust in the Word of God and his promises.
To believe in someone is to believe his words and deeds.
Faith is to walk the steps of obedience.
The most simple and most intelligent has the same way to go — the way of humbleness —
and everyone must act according to the pattern of love God has put into our hearts and
and to follow the map God has given us in His Word, with the Holy Ghost as our compass.
Faith demands courage.
Faith is to me also a product of the influence of the love of God on my will, my conscience, my mind and my emotions.

AND AS PAUL WRITES: NOW FAITH IS THE SUBSTANCE OF THINGS HOPED FOR, THE EVIDENCE OF THINGS NOT SEEN

"NOT BY
MIGHT
NOR BY
POWER
BUT BY
MY SPIRIT"

THE LORD

I will comfort them
and be their escort.
I will lead them
to flowing streams.
The Lord.

Today
if you hear
God's voice
speaking to you,
do not harden
your hearts against him.

Hebr. 3:15